FIGHTING BULLIES, HUNTING DRAGONS

STORY
JACK BRIGLIO
ART
ALEXANDER SERRA

DADDY!

GROWING UP ENCHANTED

STORY BY:
JACK BRIGLIO

ART BY:
ALEXANDER SERRA

COVER COLOURS:
JASON MILLET

LETTERING:
JUSTIN STEWART

FOR MARKOSIA ENTERPRISES, LTD.

HARRY MARKOS
PUBLISHER & MANAGING PARTNER

HUW-J
ART DIRECTOR

IAN SHARMAN
GROUP EDITOR

 Published by Markosia Enterprises, Ltd. Unit A10, Caxton Way, Stevenage, UK FIRST PRINTING, March 2010. Harry Markos, Director. Huw-J, Art Director. Printed in the UK.

ISBN: 978-1-905692-38-5

What kid wouldn't love to live in a world populated by playful dragons, helpful giants, and friendly trolls? Who wouldn't want a brave knight for a father? Or a mother who could perform sorcery? I can actually think of a number of adults who'd love all the above too. Fortunately, you hold in your hands a way to enter such a magical realm and live vicariously through a plucky little girl named Olianna.

As the title suggests, *Growing Up Enchanted* is about the life of a child living in a world of fantasy. We meet Olianna on the eve of her first day of school, but naturally she'd rather go on a dragon hunting expedition with her father the next day. Wouldn't you? But as the knightly father and magic-using daughter's adventures diverge from there, we discover that this is a story not only about Olianna but her whole family as well. It's also about their extended family, including her father's bungling fellow knights, a barbarian uncle and oracle aunt, plus schoolmates who are the aforementioned helpful giant and friendly troll. The dragon comes later. Or I should say *dragons*.

Olianna's journey to this collection has been as colorful and surprising, bumpy and fun, as her adventure within these pages. Writer Jack Briglio (whose most recent credits include *Scooby Doo* and *The Adventures of Digger and Friends*) first created the character for a scene written for a scriptwriting class in college, and later put her on a couple of short adventures within an anthology called *Mythography*, before finally casting her as the star of this book.

To help him grow and enchant the character, Jack enlisted the help of his artist friend Alex Szewczuk (whose most recent credits include *Teen Titans Go* and *Legion of Super-Heroes in the 31st Century*). Alex was just coming off of another fantastic miniseries, *Sleeping Dragons*, for which he was nominated for the Russ Manning "Most Promising Newcomer" Award.

This series itself was nominated for an Eisner Award in 2003 in the "Best Title for a Younger Audience" category (the same year as *Herobear and the Kid* and *Amelia Rules*). And just as it tells the story of Olianna's whole family, it's an all-ages tale that can also be enjoyed by the whole family. Jack has written a charming tale full of amusing characters. Alex channels Jeff Smith and Charles Vess in the art. It's a one-two combination that leaves you wanting more.

So, if you're a kid or kid at heart who wouldn't mind living in a world of dragons, giants, and friendly trolls – or at least reading about such a world – don't just sit there, turn the page already. When you get to the end, and are left wanting more (as I'm sure you will), make sure to let Jack and Alex know. Perhaps together we can convince them to revisit Olianna's family and bring us along for the ride…

J. TORRES
Toronto, Ontario
February 2010

J. Torres is the writer of Alison Dare (another Eisner "Best Title for a Younger Audience" nominee), Batman: The Brave and the Bold and WALL-E among other all-ages comic book adventures.

CHAPTER ONE...
The Baby Sorceress

GROWING UP ENCHANTED

OOOO..
MY HEAD.
SHOULD WE TELL HIM?
NO, WE SHOULDN'T.
WE HAVE TO TELL HIM.
AAAAA....
YOU KNOW HOW HE GETS, SAMMIE.
GROAN
WHAT DO YOU THINK HE'LL SAY WHEN WE TELL HIM THE NEWS?
HE'LL TELL US HOW MUCH WE SUCK.
ESPECIALLY YOU, COPPER.
YEAH, YEAH, ISH ALWAYS MY FAULT.
THE "GREAT" KANDU AND SAMMIE'S EXPERTISE UNDERMINED ONCE AGAIN BY USELESS KNIGHT-EXTRAORDINAIRE: COPPER!
YOU SAID IT, NOT ME.
SO WE'RE AGREED THEN! WE'LL TELL PANAS IT WAS ALL YOUR FAULT.
MINE AND MINE ALONE.
OOOO...
MY HEAD...

WUMP!
COPPER?
THAT LOOKS PAINFUL. YOU OKAY, COPPER?
GEEZ, COPPER!
YOU'RE SUPPOSED TO RIDE A HORSE, NOT THE OTHER WAY AROUND.
OW!
HELP
OW!
PLEASE...
SHOULD WE?
SHOULD WE WHAT?
OW! OW! OW!

YOU KNOW, HELP HIM...
HAHAHAHA
HAHAHA HEH
GIGGLE
HEHEHEH
HAHA HAHEHE
OW!
OOF.
OUCH.
OOOOOH... WHY DID WE HAVE TO MEET UP WITH THOSE DRAGONS?
UGH.
?
?
?

RRRAAAAA-
AAARRRRGH!

DRAGON!
DRAGON BAD!
R-R-RAAA!
OW!
OW!
OW!
ARF!!
ARF!!
KNIGHTS!
MOMMY!
MOMMY!
MOMMY!

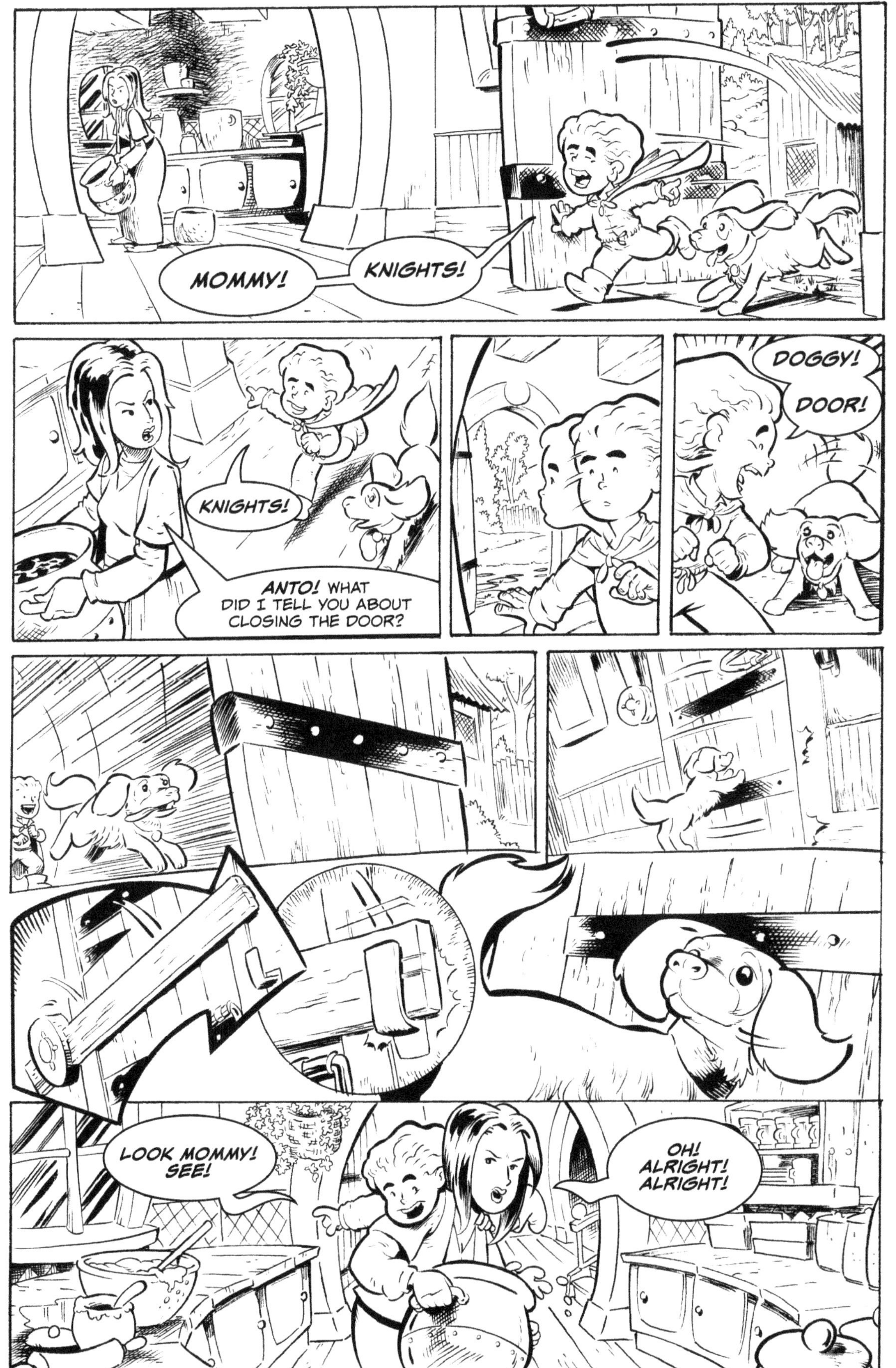
MOMMY!
KNIGHTS!
KNIGHTS!
ANTO! WHAT DID I TELL YOU ABOUT CLOSING THE DOOR?
DOGGY!
DOOR!
LOOK MOMMY! SEE!
OH! ALRIGHT! ALRIGHT!

OH GREAT.
PANAS!
WAKE UP!
PAH-NAS! WIK UP!
ANTO... PLEASE!
KNOCK! KNOCK!
BENA!!
GET THE DOOR.
IT'S *YOUR* FRIENDS, *YOU* GET THE DOOR!
KNOCK!
KNOCK!
KNOCK!
GRRRRRRRR
WHY ME?
THIS IS WHAT YOU GET FOR PROTECTING YOUR LAND? A LITTLE SLEEP TOO MUCH TO ASK?
I GUESS SO!
GRRRRRRRRRR.

RRRRRR
KNOCK! KNOCK!
DADDY!
DADDY!
KNIGHTS DADDY!
KNIGHTS! KNIGHTS!
FIGHT! FIGHT!
FIGHT!
WAM
BENA!
GET THE DOOR!
PLEASE!
SNIFF! SNIFF!
KNOCK! KNOCK!
KNOCK!
PANAS, LOOK, YOU'RE NOT GOING TO BELIEVE IT!
DRAGONS, PANAS!
I'M SORRY BIG GUY.
YOU SHOULD HAVE SEEN IT!
...OR MAYBE NOT.
YEAH, COPPER'S SORRY PANAS.
IT WAS ALL HIS FAULT.

?
WHAT? WHAT DID WE DO?
YEAH, WE HAVEN'T EVEN TOLD YOU WHAT HAPPENED YET.
IT'S NOT YOU GUYS, IT'S...
"...MY DAUGHTER...
"...OLIANNA."
WHAT?
NO ONE WANTED TO ANSWER THE DOOR.
SO I DID.

SNIFF
SNIFF
WHAT HAVE YOU BEEN TOLD ABOUT USING YOUR MAGIC, YOUNG LADY?
THEY DIDN'T SEE ME...
BUT THEY CAN SMELL IT...
DID WE COME AT A BAD TIME? WE... OOO!
WHOA!
SNIFF SNIFF
SNIFF SNIFF

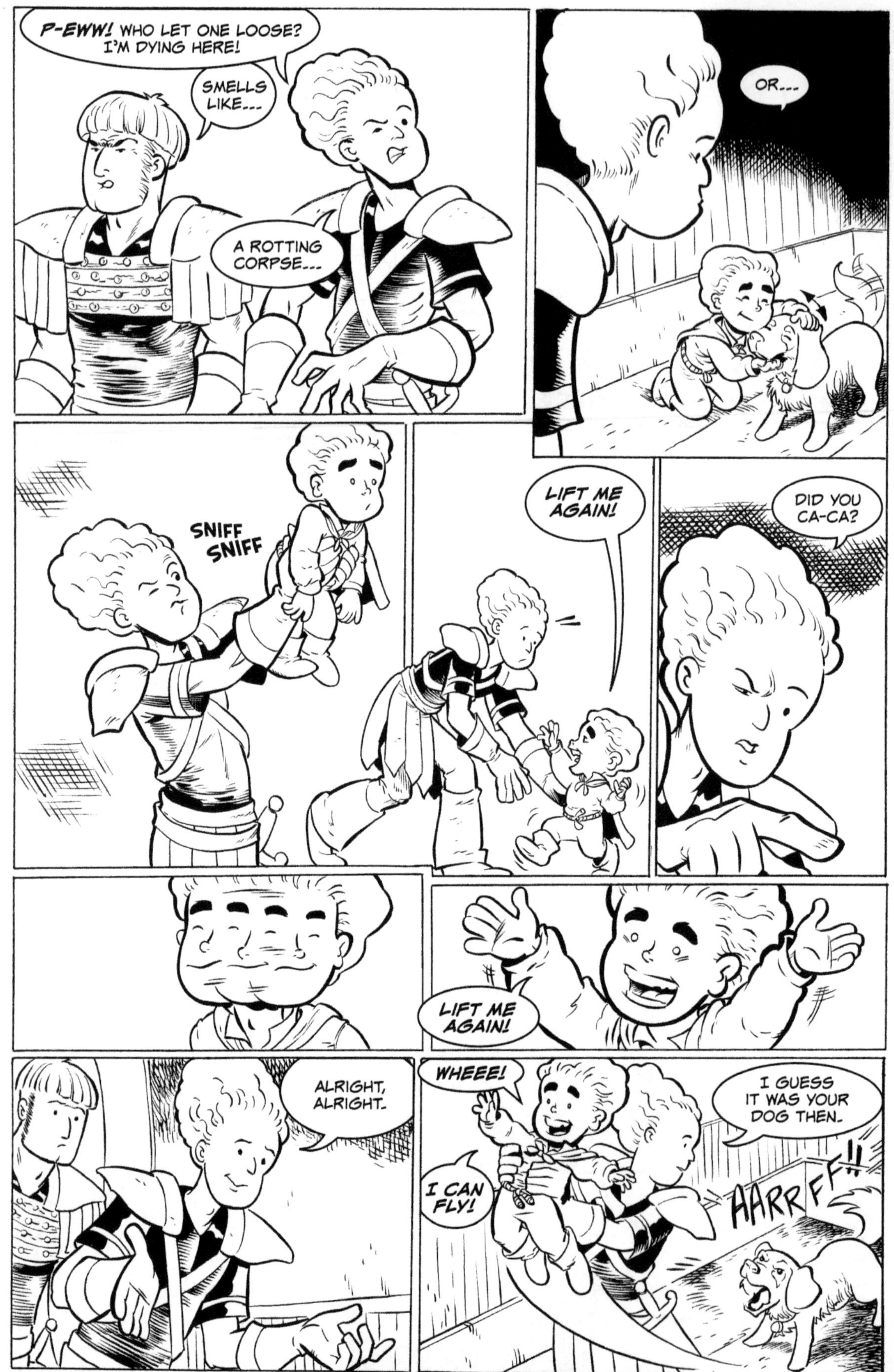
P-EWW! WHO LET ONE LOOSE? I'M DYING HERE!
SMELLS LIKE...
A ROTTING CORPSE...
OR...
SNIFF SNIFF
LIFT ME AGAIN!
DID YOU CA-CA?
LIFT ME AGAIN!
ALRIGHT, ALRIGHT.
WHEEE!
I CAN FLY!
I GUESS IT WAS YOUR DOG THEN.
AARRFF!!

WHAT'S YOUR DOG'S NAME?
DOG!
ARRF
YEAH, YOUR DOG.
DOG!
ARRF
DOG?
DOG!
ARF
OH! "DOG"!
DOG! DOG! DOG!
ARF ARF ARF
WHAT A FUNNY NAME.
COME ON GUYS, LET'S HEAD OUTSIDE SO YOU CAN FILL ME IN ON WHAT'S BOTHERING YOU...
...THIS TIME.

Later
YOU SHOULD HAVE SEEN IT PANAS.
IT WAS THIS BIG!
AND SOOOO SCARY!
OH.
REMEMBER, LITTLE LADY! NO MAGIC TRICKS!
YOU HAD TOLD US THAT AN EVIL DRAGON HAD BEEN SIGHTED AT SISCO LAKE, SO WE THOUGHT, "HEY, WHY DON'T WE START THERE? WE'RE NOT STUPID."
YEAH, WE PICK UP ON THESE THINGS.
WE KNEW WE HAD A LOT OF GROUND TO COVER IN THAT AREA, SO WE STARTED LOOKING IN THE MOST OBVIOUS SPOTS FOR THAT DRAGON.

THIS INTENSIVE SEARCH LED TO SOME-- UH---
UNFORSEEN--- UH-- TECHNICAL DIFFICULTIES-
BUT THAT DIDN'T SLOW US DOWN-
THAT ONLY STRENGTHENED OUR RESOLVE TO FIND THAT DRAGON-
HELP! I'M DROWING!
OH, SHUT UP COPPER- THE WATER'S BARELY KNEE HIGH- JUST GIVE ME YOUR HAND AND STAND UP-
UGH! I CAN HARDLY MOVE IN THIS WET ARMOR-
CREAK
CREAK
SQUEAK
AND FIND THAT DRAGON WE DID!
WUMP!

WE FOUGHT VALIANTLY, PANAS. YOU WOULD HAVE BEEN PROUD OF US.
WE ATTACKED **AND** PARRIED.

ATTACKED AND PARRIED.
PARRIED AND ATTACKED.
PANAS, IT WAS A BEAUTY TO BEHOLD.
SQUEAK?
AAAAAAAAAAA
ANTO! LEAVE YOUR SISTER ALONE. OLI! GET BACK HERE!
IT GOT WORSE THOUGH, PANAS, MUCH WORSE.
FROM OUT OF NOWHERE, A GROUP OF PRECIOUS DRAGONS JOIN THE FRAY.
THREE MORE DRAGONS, MAYBE FAMILY - WHO KNOWS? WHAT I DO KNOW IS THAT WE WERE UP TO OUR EYES IN TROUBLE.
SSSSSSSSSSSSSSS

IT WAS UTTER CHAOS!
WE WERE LUCKY TO ESCAPE WITH OUR LIVES.

GYAAAAAAAA!

WE WERE OVERWHELMED. I LOST MY HELMET DURING THE FIGHT I'M EMBARRASSED TO SAY.
PING!
NYAAAAAAA

WHOA!
CRACK
OW! OW! OW!
BINK
BONK!

YAAAAA!
AAAAAA!
WOOOM
AAAAAAAAAAA
I'M SORRY, PANAS.
AAAAAA!
WE DID OUR BEST.
THEY KNOW WE'RE AFTER THEM NOW.
YEAH! I THINK WE PUT THE FEAR OF WHATEVER DEVIL THEY WORSHIP IN THEM AT LEAST.

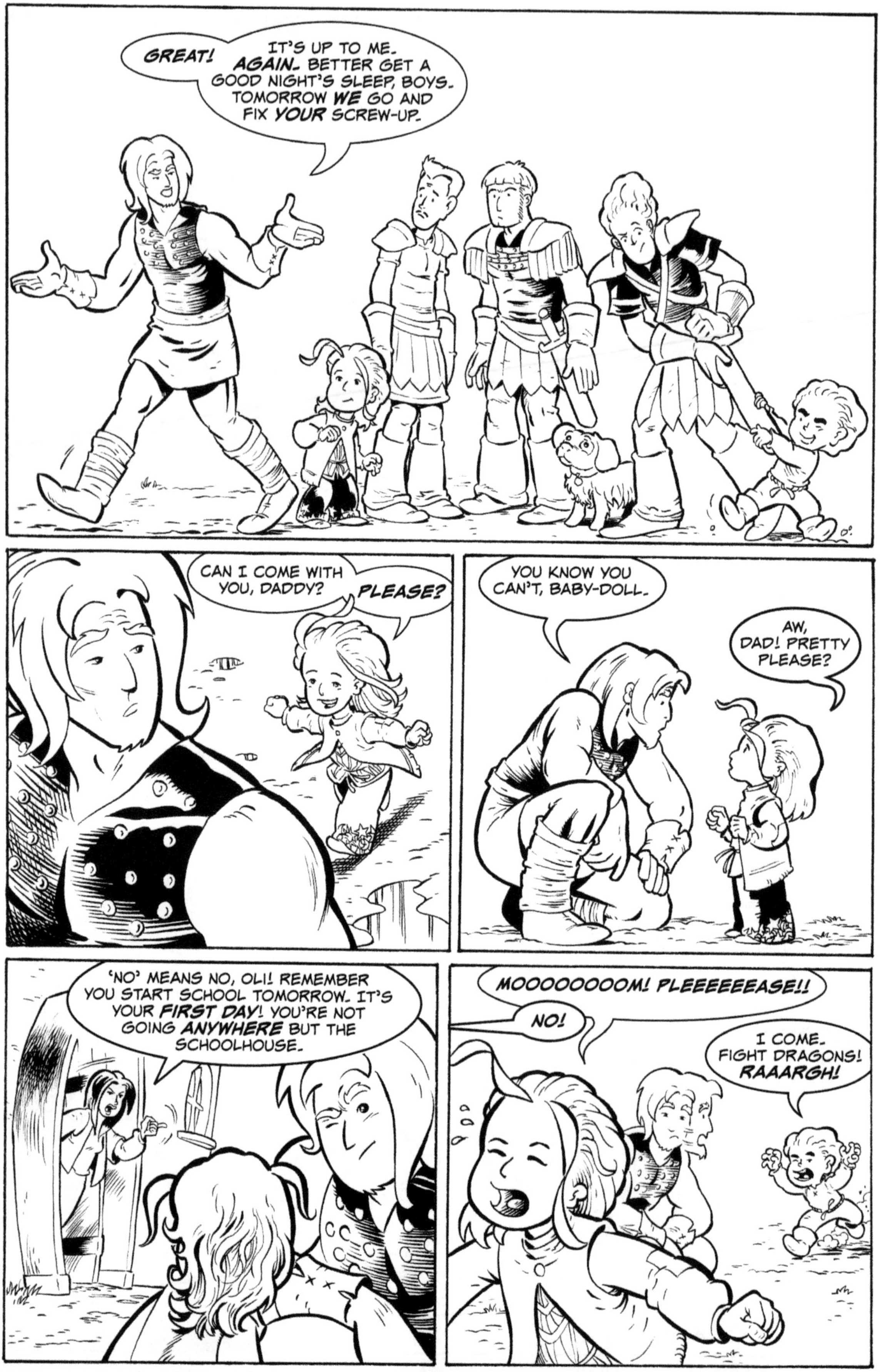

GREAT!
IT'S UP TO ME. AGAIN. BETTER GET A GOOD NIGHT'S SLEEP, BOYS. TOMORROW WE GO AND FIX YOUR SCREW-UP.

DRAGONNNNS!
WAM
ANTO! STOP!! GET OFF!
PLEASE, MOMMY. PLEASE!
NO! NO! NO!
DRAGONS! FIGHT!
WAHHH! I DON'T WANNA GO TO SCHOOL!
LISTEN HERE, YOUNG LADY...
RRRARRGH!
OW!
the next morning...
COCK-A-DOODLE-DOOo
WHO FEELS LIKE HAVING EGGS AND BACON?
ENOUGH OF THAT FACE, OLI.

YOU'RE GOING TO HAVE FUN AT SCHOOL. I'M *SURE* OF IT!
BUT DRAGONS ARE MORE FUN!
HMMF!
SPLAT!
HEEHE HEEHEH HHEHE HEE..
UH-OH.
?!?!
SPLOOT!
SHOULDN'T YOU BE HEADING OUT SOON? WE DON'T WANT OLI TO BE LATE ON HER FIRST DAY.
YUMMY. YUMMY..YUMMY YUMMY..FOR MY TUMMY.
YEAH, YEAH! I'M JUST WAITING FOR THE GUYS.
OW!

?
WHOA!
OW!
OKAY, TIME TO GO! YOU READY, OLI?
I GUESS.
SHLUURP!
Later
ALL SET, OLI?
AW, YOU'LL BE FINE.
THE DAY WILL FLY BY. JUST YOU WAIT.
AND REMEMBER WHAT YOUR MOMMA TOLD YOU ABOUT USING MAGIC.
ANTO!
STOP!
I SAID STOP!

moments later...
OLI!
WANNA GO WITH OLI!
a little later again...

a little later still...

HEY, THERE'S PAUL! HIS SON GOES HERE TOO! SEE, OLI? THERE'S YOUR FIRST FRIEND.
DOESN'T HE HUNT DRAGONS WITH YOU?
YEAH, USUALLY.
JUST NOT WITH THESE BOZOS, YOU UNDER-STAND?
ON THE HORSE COPPER!
STUPID TREE...
GO ON OVER THERE AND TALK TO PAUL'S SON.
THEY'RE A NICE FAMILY. AND I'LL TRY TO GET THIS HUNT STUFF OVER WITH AS SOON AS I CAN, OKAY?

WISH ME LUCK.
GOOD LUCK, DADDY!

CHAPTER TWO...
Fighting Bullies, Hunting Dragons

MOMMY? WHO RIDES IN THERE?
THAT'S THE ROYAL CARRIAGE, SON. I IMAGINE ONE OF YOUR FELLOW STUDENTS MAY BE THE PRINCE HIMSELF.
SNAP!
AND THAT'S THE CARRIAGE DRIVER. HE'S...UH...
LET'S NEVER MIND WHO THAT IS... YOU JUST...JUST TURN AWAY.
WHY MOMMY? WHO IS HE?
I SAID NEVERMIND! WHY DON'T YOU JUST GO AND MEET THE REST OF YOUR CLASS!?
BUT..?

THERE'S A LOT MORE THAN YOUR JOBS RIDING ON THAT BOY'S SAFETY, AM I UNDERSTOOD?
AYE, SIR. YOU CAN COUNT ON US.

YOU'RE FUNNY LOOKING.
HMMFF!!
YOU'RE NOT AFRAID OF ME, ARE YOU?
I BROKE MY NOSE IN A FIGHT ONCE.
SEE...
THWUNG
WUBBA-WUBBA--WUBBA--

PRETTY GOOD, EH?
YOU'RE SCARED OF ME, AREN'T YOU?
RARRGH!
YAAA!
BANG! BANG!
WAHH!
OLIANNA!
I SAID NO MAGIC!
POOF
CLANG
HEY!
SCHOOL'S STARTED!
!?!

OOOF!
GRRR...
STOMP
STOMP
PLOP
WHAT?!
COME ON IN... OLIANNA IS IT? WE'RE ALL FRIENDS HERE.
I'M NOT HER FRIEND! I'M NO GIRL'S FRIEND.
GLAD TO HEAR IT.

WATCH IT, YOU.
?
COME. WE'LL FIND YOU A PLACE TO SIT.

OLI--BOWLI-- SLOWLY...
THAT'S ENOUGH, CHAD.
HMM.
OLI...WALKS SLOWLY. OLI IS SLOWLY, VERY LOWLY...
OLI LIVES IN A BOWLY.
JUST ONE LITTLE OGRE... JUST ONE TO MAKE HIM WET HIS SLIMY, ICKY PANTS.
HEE HEEHE
?!
COULD YOU STOP, PLEASE?
DON'T YOU MEAN, "PRETTY PLEASE WITH A CHERRY ON TOP"?

STOP IT, YOU TWO! THIS ISN'T A GOOD START TO THE FIRST DAY OF SCHOOL NOW, IS IT?
THAT'S BETTER.
NOW, LET'S BEGIN CLASS TODAY BY DOING SOME DRAWINGS. I'M WILLING TO BET YOU'RE A TALENTED BUNCH.
YAY! CHALK!
ONE FOR YOU.
THANK YOU.
I'M GOING TO DRAW A DRAGON.
ME TOO.
CRUMPLE
CRINKLE

TWAP
RRRRRRRR R...
NYAHH-LA, LA LA
BUMP
YEOOW!
HO!
HA! HA!
HO!
HA! HO!
HA!
HA!
WWAAAAR

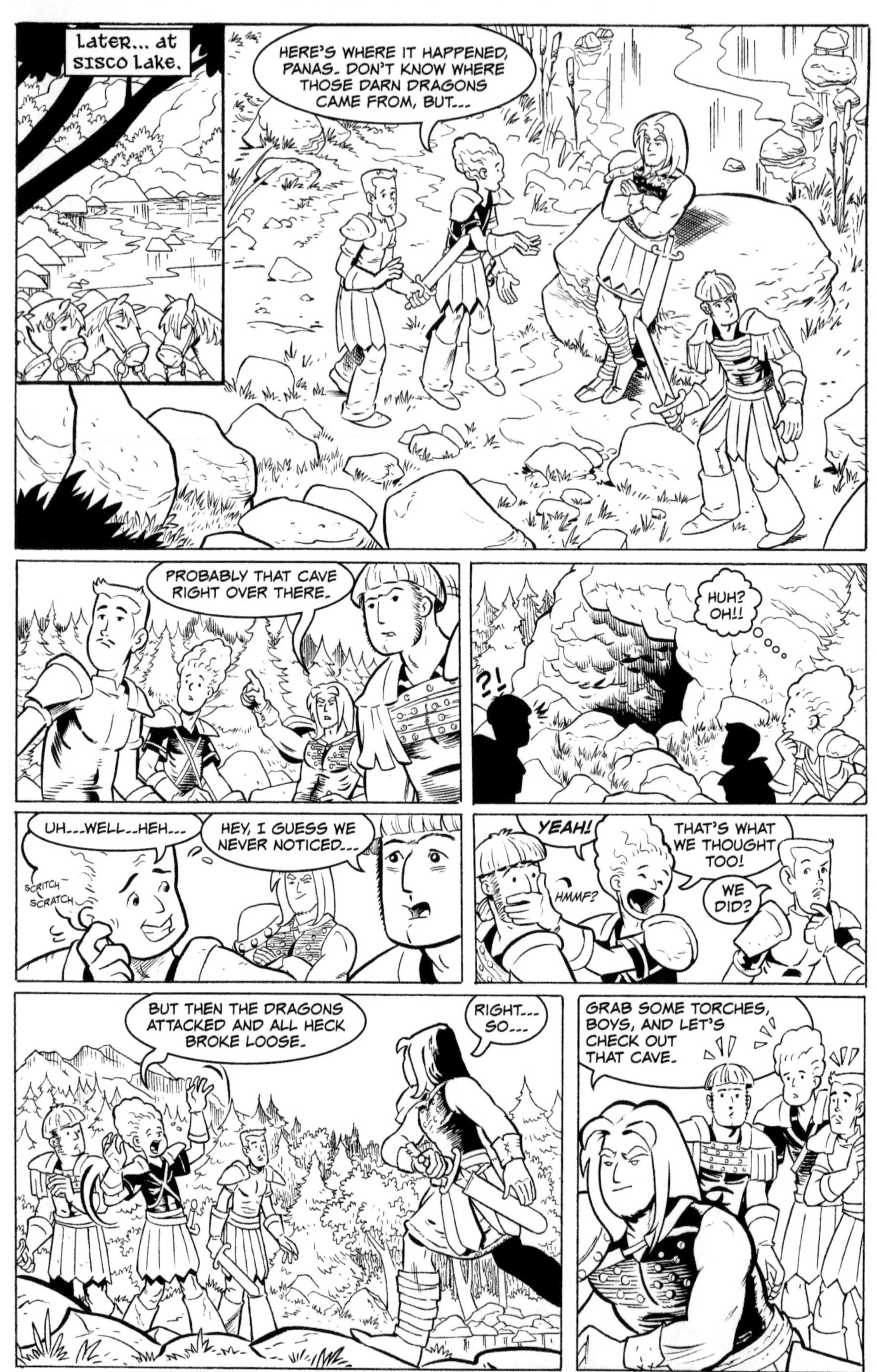
Later... at SISCO Lake.
HERE'S WHERE IT HAPPENED, PANAS. DON'T KNOW WHERE THOSE DARN DRAGONS CAME FROM, BUT...
PROBABLY THAT CAVE RIGHT OVER THERE.
?!
HUH? OH!!
UH...WELL..HEH...
SCRITCH SCRATCH
HEY, I GUESS WE NEVER NOTICED...
YEAH!
HMMF?
THAT'S WHAT WE THOUGHT TOO!
WE DID?
BUT THEN THE DRAGONS ATTACKED AND ALL HECK BROKE LOOSE.
RIGHT... SO...
GRAB SOME TORCHES, BOYS, AND LET'S CHECK OUT THAT CAVE.

YOU FIRST.
NO, YOU.
YEAH...
PLEASE... I INSIST, YOU!
?
I SAID NO! YOU!
HEY!
THEN YOU GO.
YEAH! YOU GO.
YOU SHUT UP!!
OH, YEAH?!
YOU ASKED FOR IT!

Back at school...
...during recess.
HMM?
UMMMM...
THANKS.
AWWW.
HE DESERVED IT! I SAVED YOU THE TROUBLE.

SAVED ME GETTING *INTO* TROUBLE, YOU MEAN.
YEAH!
MY NAME IS BRADLEY.
YOU'RE OLIANNA, RIGHT?
PLEASED TO MEETCHA!
EVERYONE'S AFRAID TO COME UP TO ME BECAUSE I'M SO TALL, BUT I LIKE TO PLAY JUST LIKE EVERYONE ELSE.
SO THEN...
LET'S PLAY!
HA HA!
Back at the cave...
NOTHING.
THEY'RE LONG GONE.

PHEW!
OH YEAH!
I THOUGHT WE WERE DEAD FOR SURE.
WE'LL START FRESH AGAIN TOMORROW. I'M GOING TO ASK A FRIEND OF MINE TO COME ALONG. HE'S AN EXPERT TRACKER. HE'LL HELP US FIND THOSE DRAGONS.
"US?" UMM. ARE YOU SURE YOU WANT US TO COME WITH YOU TOMORROW?
YEAH, DO YOU REALLY NEED US WITH THAT EXPERT TRACKER COMING?
OF COURSE I WANT YOU TO COME. I WOULDN'T WANT TO TAKE AWAY ALL YOUR GLORY. STEAL YOUR THUNDER. THIS IS YOUR HUNT.
NO, IT'S OKAY, REALLY. WE BELIEVE IN TEAMWORK. DON'T WE, GUYS?!
WE SURE DO! WE DON'T BELIEVE IN HOGGING THE SPOTLIGHT. NO, SIR!
AND?
...AND...
UH...
...AND WELL...
...UH.
...AND SAMMIE'S MOM IS HAVING US OVER FOR DINNER TONIGHT AND SHE'S A REALLY EXCELLENT COOK AND WE'RE REALLY NOT GOING TO BE IN ANY SHAPE TO, YOU KNOW, HUNT. TOMORROW'S SUPPOSED TO BE OUR DAY OFF AND WE'VE BEEN LOOKING FORWARD TO THIS DINNER ALL WEEK AND...
AND I HAVE A FAMILY TO TAKE CARE OF, BUT YOU DON'T SEE ME HIDING BEHIND THAT EXCUSE OR COMPLAINING FOR THAT MATTER.
YOU BROUGHT ME INTO THIS HUNT, REMEMBER?

BUT SHE'S A REALLY GOOD COOK.
WE'LL BRING YOU THE LEFTOVERS. WHAT D'YA SAY?
GRRR
MUMBLE STUPID GRUMBLE..
FIRST THING TOMORROW! YOU TWITS BETTER BE READY!
THAT WENT WELL.
I THINK PANAS KNEW THAT TOO, DIMWIT.
WE NEVER LEAVE ANY LEFTOVERS, COPPER.
that night olianna's family gathers for dinner, joined by uncle jed, a barbarian, and aunt gigi, an oracle.
SO OLI, HOW WAS YOUR FIRST DAY OF SCHOOL?
OKAY, I GUESS.
JUST OKAY?
JUST OKAY.
WHAT HAPPENED?
A BOY WAS MEAN TO ME TODAY. HE WAS MAKING FUN OF ME AND CALLING ME NAMES..
NOT BRADLEY?!
NO. HE'S NICE. THIS BOY'S A BIG, BAD BULLY. CHAD. CHAD THE BAD.

WOW - QUITE A NICKNAME. DID YOU STAND UP TO HIM?
HOW COULD I? MOMMY SAID NOT TO USE ANY OF MY MAGIC.
OH, HOW I WANTED TO SIC AN OGRE ON CHAD. THAT WOULD HAVE TAUGHT HIM A LESSON.
BUT NOOOOO--- I WASN'T ALLOWED.
JUST BECAUSE YOU CAN'T USE YOUR MAGIC, OLIANNA, DOESN'T MEAN YOU CAN'T STAND UP TO THE LITTLE THUG! THERE ARE OTHER WAYS. SNEAKIER WAYS. HELL HATH NO FURY...
---THAN AN OLIANNA SPURNED!
GO INTO SCHOOL TOMORROW, OLIANNA, AND CHALLENGE "CHAD THE BAD" TO A DUEL. AFTER YOU CLEAN HIS CLOCK, PLACE HIS CARCASS ON DISPLAY FOR THE WORLD TO SEE.
SERIOUSLY, THOUGH, OLIANNA, DON'T BACK DOWN. BULLIES BULLY WHO THEY THINK ARE WEAK. YOU'RE NOT WEAK. STAND UP TO HIM AND HE'LL BACK DOWN. I'M SURE OF IT.
YOU KNOW I DON'T TELL MY PROPHECIES BUT I'LL TELL YOU THIS, OLIANNA - JUST IGNORE THAT IMMATURE BULLY. YOU'RE BETTER THAN THAT.

AUNT GIGI'S RIGHT. FIGHTING'S NO GOOD. IT NEVER GETS YOU ANYWHERE. TRUST ME - UNCLE JED KNOWS.
FIGHT! FIGHT! FIGHT!
WELL, I THINK WE ALL HAVE MADE SOME GOOD POINTS TONIGHT.
YUP. I AGREE. CLEAR AS MUD, OLIANNA.
??
RIGHT.
the next day...
WHAT'S WRONG WITH YOU GUYS THIS TIME?
OOOO - MOM DECIDED TO TRY OUT SOME NEW SPICES... UGH... THAT SOME MERCHANT FROM DOWN SOUTH SOLD HER... AND.. UH... THEY AREN'T SITTING WITH US SO WELL, I GOTTA TELL.. OH... YOU.
THEY TASTED GREAT GOING DOWN... OOO... BUT THEY DON'T WANNA STAY IN. WE HAD TO STOP FOR TWO TOILET BREAKS JUST GETTING... UGH... HERE.
RUMBLE GRUMBLE
GURGLE
BLURBLE

YOU. GUYS. ARE. IDIOTS!
THAT'S NOT FAIR. IT WAS SO GOO... UH... OOOH... UH-OH.
BURBLE
GURGLE
OOO... STOMACH... OOOH... OH...
OH...
OOH... HURRY... HURRY... HURRY.
OH. THIS IS GOING TO BE A GREAT DAY.
HEY... WHERE'S ANTO?
HE MUST'VE TIRED HIMSELF OUT YESTERDAY. I COULDN'T GET HIM OUT OF BED.
SNORE
ANTO! BREAKFAST! ANTO...?!
NOW IF ONLY HE GIVES ME A FEW HOURS OF PEACE AND QUIET.
PEACE AND QUIET. YEAH, RIGHT.
ZZZZZZ
CLICK

HEE
HEE
Later at school, Olianna's class learns how to play a game called "hot potato."
THAT'S IT, BOYS AND GIRLS, PRETEND THAT THE BALL IS ON FIRE AND IT'S TOO HOT TO TOUCH. CATCH IT AND THROW IT TO SOMEONE ELSE AS FAST AS YOU CAN. DROPPING IT MEANS YOU'RE OUT.
THAT'S IT! TRY TO PICK UP THE PACE.
WEE... WHAT FUN!
BUMP
PLOP

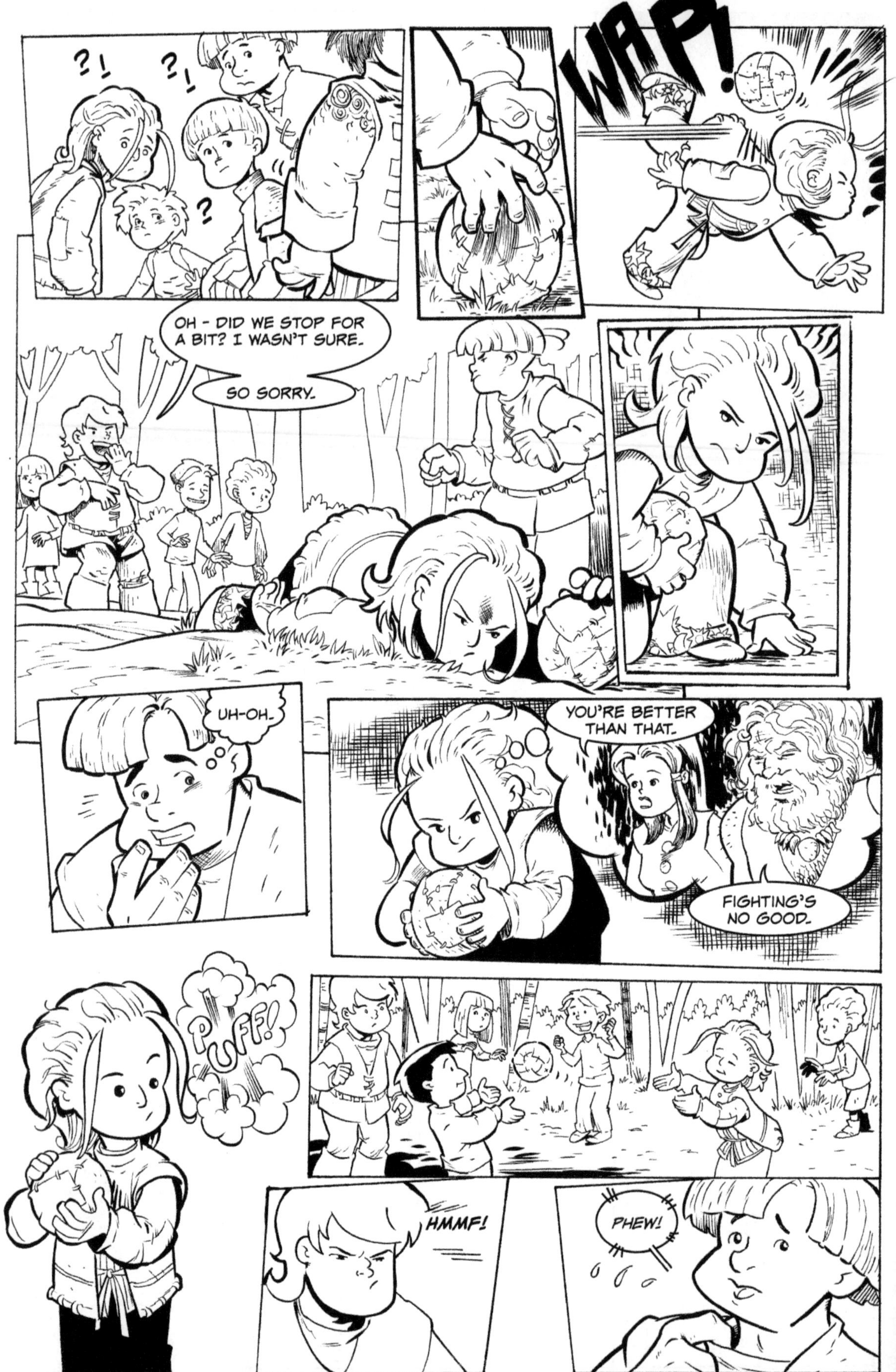
?!
?!
?
WAP!
OH - DID WE STOP FOR A BIT? I WASN'T SURE.
SO SORRY.
UH-OH.
YOU'RE BETTER THAN THAT.
FIGHTING'S NO GOOD.
PUFF!
HMMF!
PHEW!

OOOOPS. I DON'T EVEN KNOW MY OWN STRENGTH. HEH HEH.
BE CAREFUL, CHAD. YOU DON'T HAVE TO THROW IT SO HARD.
SORRY. IT WON'T HAPPEN AGAIN.
PLEASE SEE THAT IT DOESN'T.
?!
THERE ARE OTHER WAYS.
YOU'RE NOT WEAK. STAND UP TO HIM. HE'LL BACK DOWN.
I'M NOT SCARED OF YOU, CHAD! I'M WARNING YOU - DON'T PUSH ME.
YOU MEAN LIKE THIS?

YOU'VE GOT SPUNK FOR A GIRL. I LIKE THAT.
FIGHT! FIGHT! FIGHT!
SSSSSSSS
?!?
WAM!

SWOOSH
HEY, WHAT'S THAT SMELL?
WHO LIT ONE?
EWWW..
SNIFF SNIFF
WUMP
ENOUGH OF THIS NONSENSE.
OLIANNA - DETENTION AFTER SCHOOL!
PLOP
AND CHAD? YOU TOO. THE BOTH OF YOU WILL HAVE TO LEARN TO GET ALONG!
OOOOOHHH
SNIFF...EWW.
ARE YOU OKAY?
KIDS... HAVEN'T I POINTED OUT THE OUTHOUSE TO YOU YET?
I CAN'T BELIEVE I HAVE DETENTION!
IT'S NOT FAIR!
I KNOW. IT SUCKS.
I'M SICK OF THIS SCHOOL.
I'M GOING TO FIND MY DAD AND HUNT DRAGONS INSTEAD. THAT'S MORE FUN THAN THIS BALONEY! YOU WITH ME, BRADLEY?
YOU BET!
DID SOMEONE SAY DRAGONS?

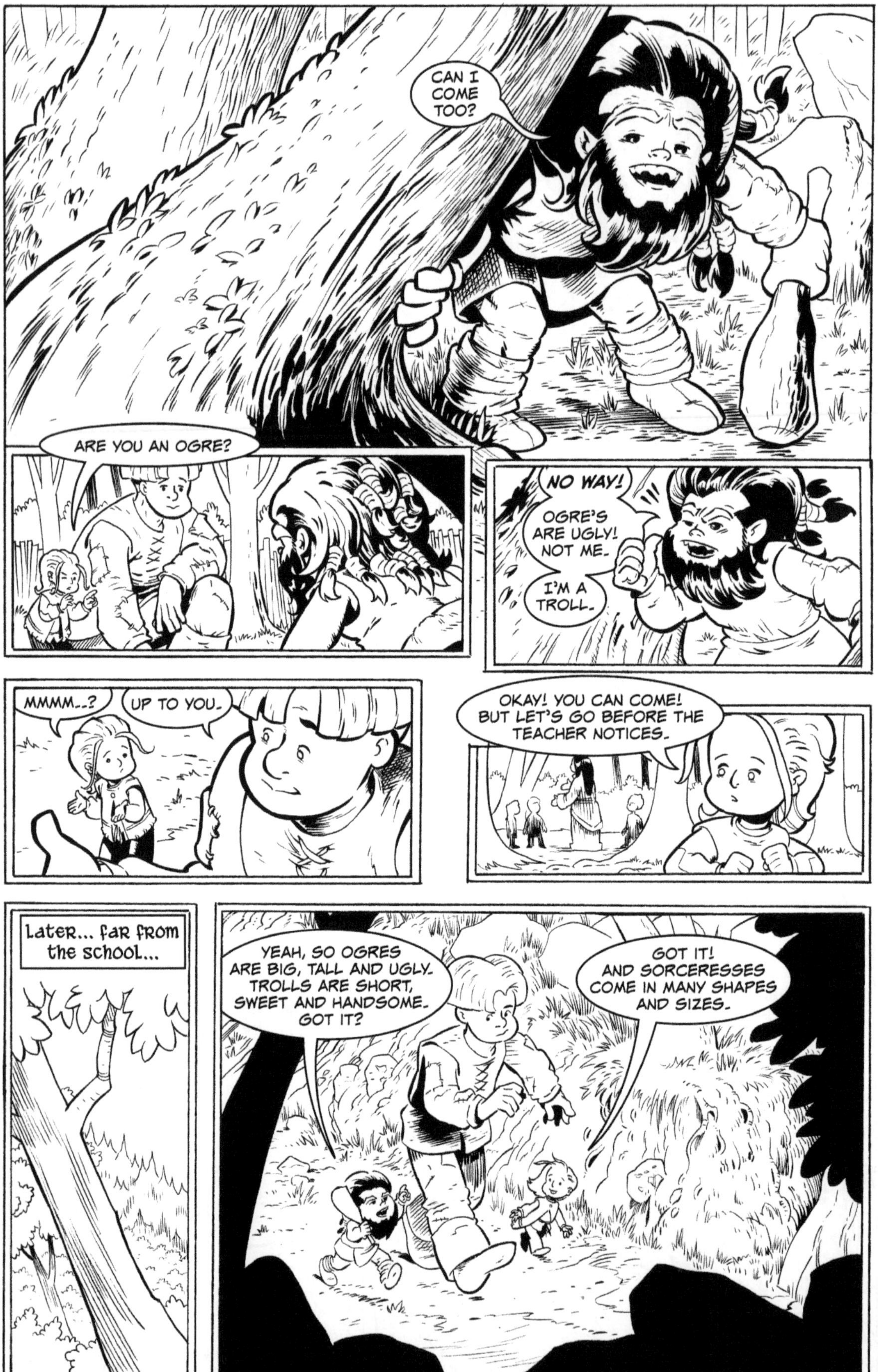

CAN I COME TOO?

ARE YOU AN OGRE?

NO WAY!

OGRE'S ARE UGLY! NOT ME.

I'M A TROLL.

AND GIANTS ARE TALL AND NICE. UNLESS YOU CLIMB THEIR BEANSTALK AND STEAL FROM THEM. WE DON'T TAKE TOO KINDLY TO THAT.
HAHA
HAHA HOHO
DO YOU THINK I WAS TOO ROUGH ON CHAD?
NO.
NOT ENOUGH.
YOU'RE LUCKY THAT MS. CRABTREE DIDN'T SUSPECT ANYTHING MAGIC ABOUT YOUR STUNT. YOU'D BE KICKED OUT OF SCHOOL.
GOOD THING ADULTS AREN'T SO SMART. NOT LIKE US KIDS.
I HOPE EVERYONE DOESN'T KNOW. MY MOM WOULD BE SO MAD. BUT MY PARENTS ARE GOING TO KILL ME, ANYWAY. SECOND DAY OF SCHOOL AND DETENTION ALREADY.
NOT TO MENTION SKIPPING SCHOOL. DON'T FORGET THAT.
I'M IN DEEP.
WE'RE IN DEEP.
WHAT ABOUT YOUR PARENTS, THOMAS? THEY GOING TO BE MAD.

WELL. UMMM...
...HEY, WHAT'S THAT?!
WHAT IS IT?
FOLLOW ME!
SEE?! THIS IS WAY MORE FUN THAN SCHOOL.
SNIFF! SNIFF!
Later...
WHERE HAVE YOU BROUGHT US, THOMAS?
YEAH, ARE WE LOST?
SNIFF! SNIFF!
YOU WANTED TO FIND SOME DRAGONS?! AM I RIGHT? WELL, COME ON. THIS WAY!!
ONWARD! I CAN FEEL IT!
WOW!
OH!

...DRAGONS!

meanwhile, panas and the three knights continue their journey to seek out the expert dragon-tracker, paul the giant.
OOO...CAN WE STOP SOON? I THINK I GOTTA GO AGAIN.
YEAH, PANAS, CAN WE STOP? MY STOMACH'S KILLING ME.
SHUT UP, YOU YAY-HOOS! WE'RE ALMOST THERE!
YOU SEE OVER THERE.
ONCE WE GO BEYOND THOSE MISTS, WE'LL FIND OURSELVES IN BINSTAULK, THE HOME OF THE GIANTS. IT'S THERE WE'LL MEET UP WITH PAUL. WITH HIS HELP WE'LL EASILY FIND YOUR DRAGONS.
I WOULD RATHER FIND A TOILET.
AWW... GIVE IT A REST.
DRAGON!!

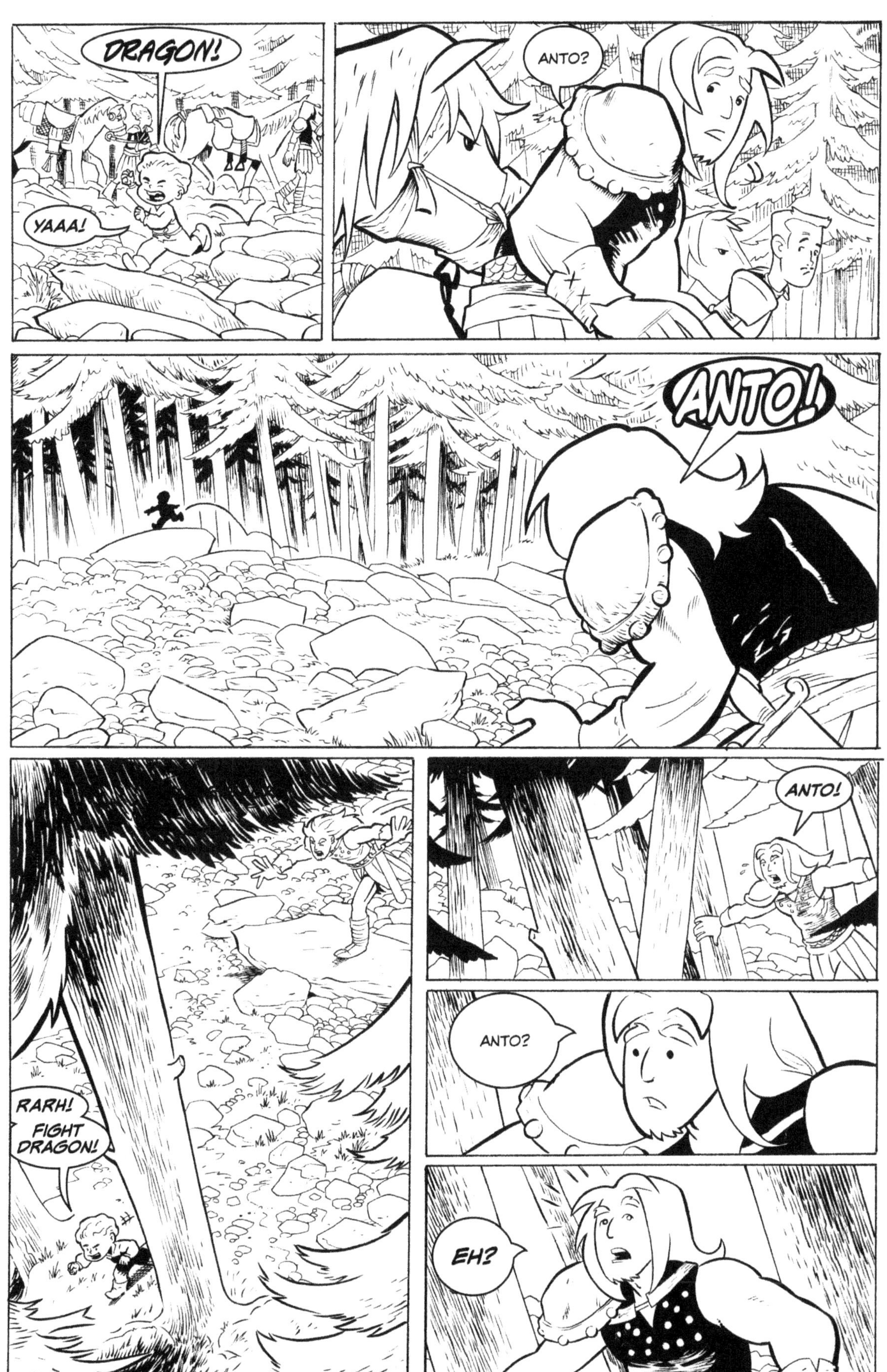
DRAGON!
YAAA!
ANTO?
ANTO!!
RARH! FIGHT DRAGON!
ANTO!
ANTO?
EH?

YAH! DRAGONS! FIIIIIGHT! FIGHT!! FIGHT!!!
ANTO!
HEY, COPPER... ISN'T THAT YOUR HELMET?
BATHROOM!! AAAAAAHH!

CHAPTER THREE...

THEY'RE GOING TO BLAME US, OF COURSE.
BLAME YOU, YOU MEAN.
YEAH.
WHAT DID WE DO?
WHAT DID I DO? IS IT MY FAULT WE CAN'T FIND THOSE DRAGONS?
IS IT MY FAULT PANAS' SON ANTO STOWED AWAY WITH HIM? THEN WAS ABDUCTED BY ONE OF THE DRAGONS WE WERE HUNTING?
YOUR HELMET LOOKED GOOD ON HIM.
IS IT MY FAULT WE'RE IN THIS MESS? NO! IT'S YOUR MOM'S FAULT, SAMMIE. YOUR MOM AND HER SECRET SPICES.
COPPER! KANDU! SAMMIE! COME ON! GET A MOVE ON IT.
HMMF! MY MOM MAKES A MEAN PASTA.
YEAH, MMMMM...
COME ON, LET'S GO. OTHERWISE, WE'LL NEVER HEAR THE END OF IT.

WE'RE TAKING TOO LONG! ANTO'S LIFE DEPENDS ON IT!
TRY NOT TO WORRY, PANAS. WE KNOW WHAT DIRECTION HE WAS TAKEN.
AND REMEMBER, DRAGONS TEND TO SETTLE IN FAMILIAR AREAS. WE KNOW THIS LAND BETTER THAN ANYONE HERE. WE'LL FIND HIM.
I HOPE SO.
MY LIFE DEPENDS ON IT AS WELL! BENA WILL HAVE MY HIDE!
OOOOO... WHEN WILL IT END?
DEAL WITH IT, GUYS!
BUT...

HOLD!
IT!
IN!
UNDERSTAND?
MUMBLE! GRUMBLE!
HOW DO WE KNOW THAT HE HASN'T HAD HIS, UM, DINNER, YET?
FORTUNATELY FOR US, DRAGONS...
"...TEND TO PLAY WITH THEIR FOOD BEFORE GORGING."
AAAAAAAAAAAAAAAAAAAAAAA

AREN'T WE SUPPOSED TO BE HUNTING DRAGONS?
YES, BUT -
THEN WHY ARE WE RUNNING?
BECAUSE THAT'S ONE, BIG...
...DRAGON!

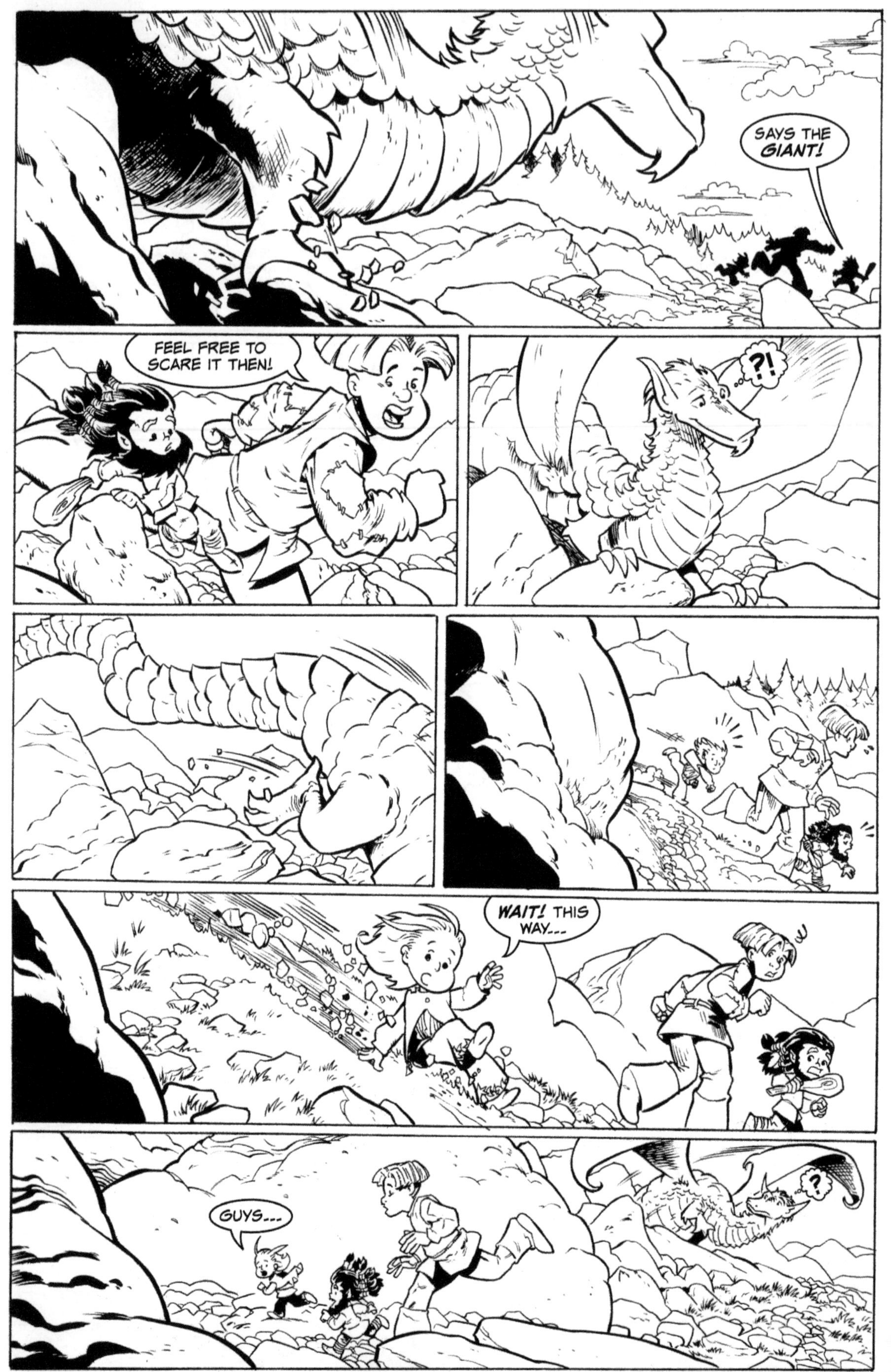
SAYS THE GIANT!
FEEL FREE TO SCARE IT THEN!
?!
WAIT! THIS WAY...
GUYS...
?

...YOU CAN LEAVE IT TO ME.
I'LL HIDE US!
SNIFF SNIFF!
EEK!
PEE-EEWWWWW
HEY! I CAN'T SEE ME.
NO! BUT I CAN SMELL YOU. OLI'S MAGIC IS SOOO STINKY.
BYE-BYE, DADDY DRAGON!
DRAGON!
ANTO FIGHT!
?!?
AH-HA!
BONK! BONK! BONK!
RRRRRR

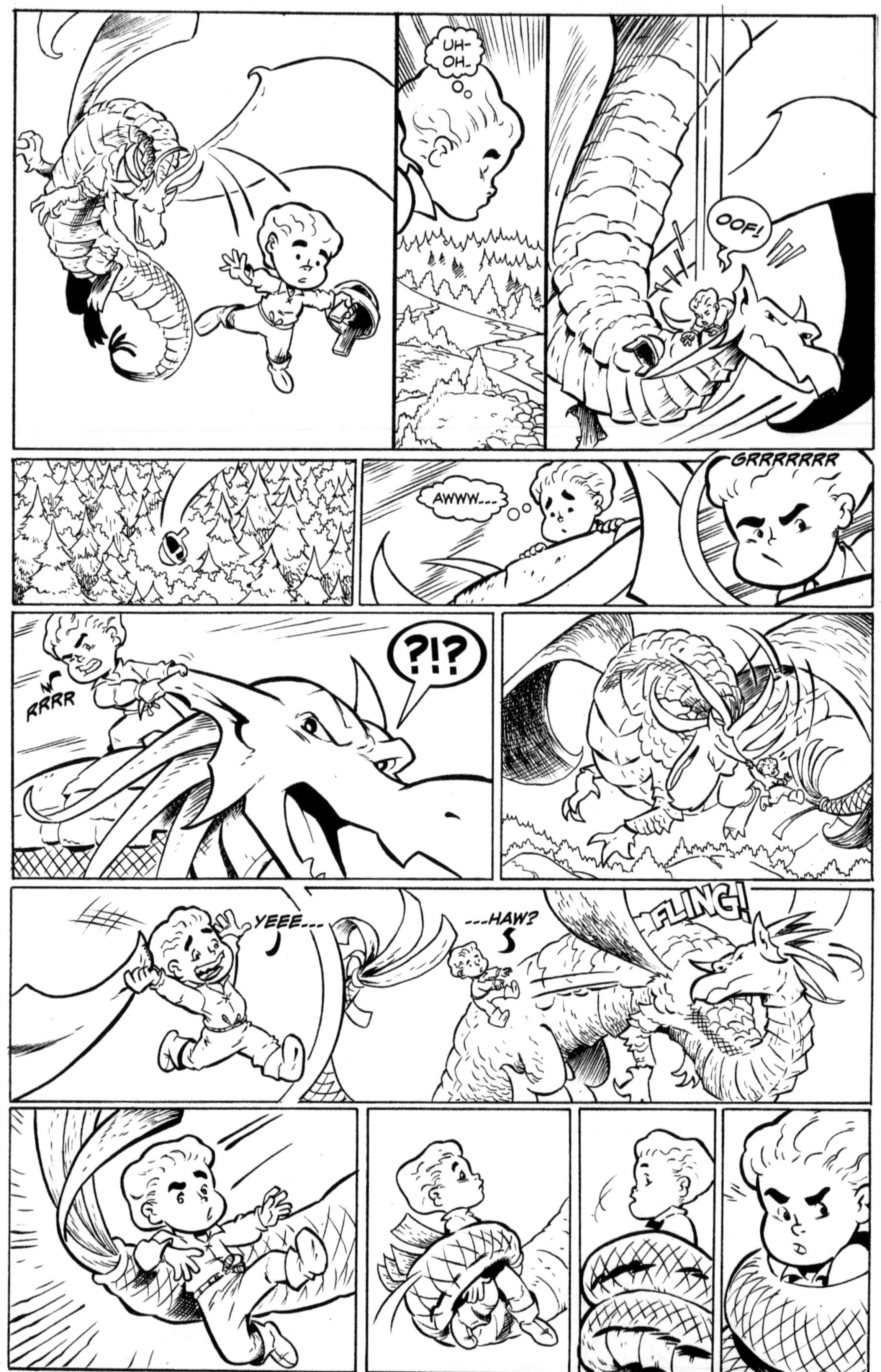
UH-OH.
OOF!
AWWW...
GRRRRRRR
RRRR
?!?
YEEE...
...HAW?
FLING!

ELSEWHERE...
WHY DO THE MISTS HAVE TO BE SO... ...SO...
MISTY?
YEAH! MISTY.
AND WHY DOES FOG HAVE TO BE SO FOGGY, RIGHT COPPER?
YEAH! WHY... OH.. UH.. NEVER MIND. COME ON, HORSEY.
WHERE ARE WE?
DOON.
DOOM!?
DOON, THE LAND OF THE DRAGONS. WHEN THEY'RE NOT HUNTING, THEY'RE HERE. AND THEY'RE HERE FOR ONE REASON ONLY: TO EAT!

PAUL, THIS LAND IS HUGE! WHERE DO WE START LOOKING FOR ANTO?
MY GUESS IS OVER THERE, COPPER.
AT THE TOP OF THAT BIG HILL.
DRAGONS TEND TO FEAST AT HIGH ALTITUDES. THAT SEEMS TO BE THE HIGHEST PEAK, SO LET'S START THERE.
LET'S GET A MOVE ON IT THEN. NO MORE WASTING TIME. WE CAN'T AFFORD IT.
YOU THINK THERE'S TIME FOR A TOILET BREAK?
NO!
Later...

GREAT! THE PATH IS BLOCKED.
OVER THERE AS WELL.
WE'LL HAVE TO CIRCLE BACK AND TRY THE OTHER SIDE.
AND HOW LONG WILL THAT TAKE?
AT LEAST ANOTHER HALF-HOUR OR MORE.
THERE MUST BE ANOTHER WAY -
UH, NO TIME FOR THAT.
THERE THEY ARE.

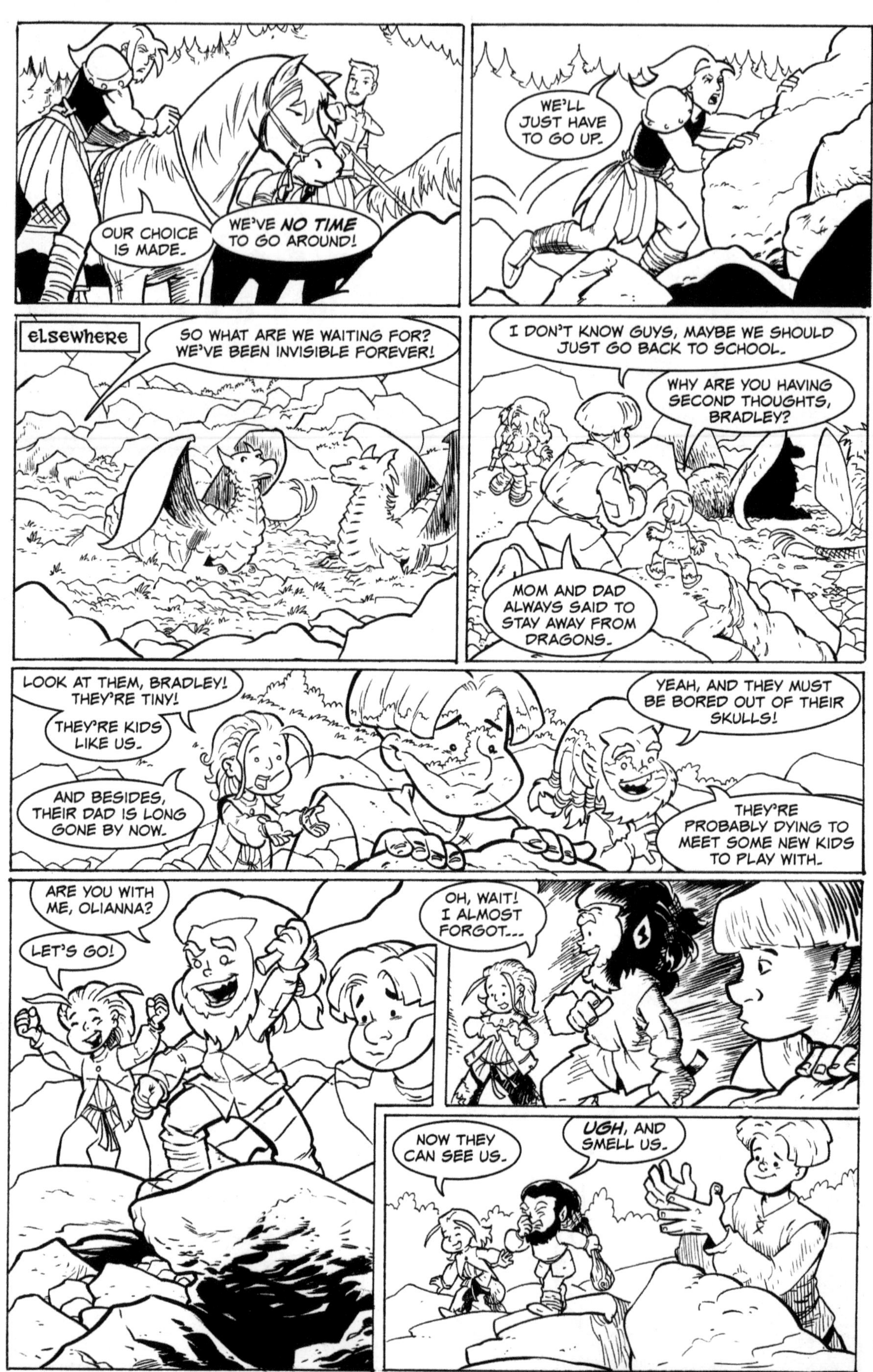

OUR CHOICE IS MADE.
WE'VE NO TIME TO GO AROUND!
WE'LL JUST HAVE TO GO UP.
ELSEWHERE
SO WHAT ARE WE WAITING FOR? WE'VE BEEN INVISIBLE FOREVER!
I DON'T KNOW GUYS, MAYBE WE SHOULD JUST GO BACK TO SCHOOL.
WHY ARE YOU HAVING SECOND THOUGHTS, BRADLEY?
MOM AND DAD ALWAYS SAID TO STAY AWAY FROM DRAGONS.
LOOK AT THEM, BRADLEY! THEY'RE TINY!
THEY'RE KIDS LIKE US.
AND BESIDES, THEIR DAD IS LONG GONE BY NOW.
YEAH, AND THEY MUST BE BORED OUT OF THEIR SKULLS!
THEY'RE PROBABLY DYING TO MEET SOME NEW KIDS TO PLAY WITH.
ARE YOU WITH ME, OLIANNA?
LET'S GO!
OH, WAIT! I ALMOST FORGOT...
NOW THEY CAN SEE US.
UGH, AND SMELL US.

---SEBASTIAN, COME BACK HERE THIS INSTANT, YOU POOR EXCUSE FOR A SON!
HELLO..?
DEAR, WHY COULDN'T HE BE MORE LIKE ROSCOE?
THEY CAN TALK?
YEAH, AND THEY DON'T SOUND LIKE KIDS.
OH LOOK DEAREST, IT'S THOSE NON-WINGED CREATURES!
WHY, HELLO NON-WINGED CREATURES!
I LIKE THEM.
YEAH, DRAGONS ARE NICE.

LET'S EAT!
YAAAAAAA
BOOOOM
OH BOY...
ANTO!?!
WHOAAAAAAAA
OLI-!! OLI-!! YAY!!

ISN'T ANTO YOUR BROTHER?
YES! AND WE HAVE TO HELP HIM!
OH NO... OUR FRIEND IS BACK!!
OH, WONDERFUL - ANOTHER NON-WINGED CREATURE FOR DINNER.
RRRRRRRRUUUUUUUMMBBLE
SCREECH!

I... I THINK YOUR MOM WAS RIGHT!
ABOUT WHAT?!
ABOUT STAYING AWAY FROM DRAGONS!

CHAPTER FOUR...
DADDY!

ANTO! I'M COMING FOR YOU, LITTLE GUY!
COME ON, GUYS - WE HAVE NO TIME TO WASTE!
WELL, BOYS, WE WANTED TO FIND DRAGONS...

---AND BOY-O-BOY, OLI, WE FOUND DRAGONS ALRIGHT!
ENOUGH TALK, BRADLEY. ISN'T THIS WHAT WE'VE BEEN WAITING FOR? WHY WE SKIPPED SCHOOL IN THE FIRST PLACE?
LET'S GET 'EM!

AAAAAAAH!
OH NO...
COME ON! BRING EVERYTHING YOU'VE GOT! I'M NOT SCARED!
LET'S PLAY!
PLAY!
PLAY!
??!
?!?
!??!?!
PLAY? P-L-A-Y. PLAY!!!
OKAY, SURE THEN, LET'S PLAY...
...HEY, WAIT A MINUTE!

?!!?
PLEASE! PLEASE! PLEASE! NEW FRIENDS, NEW FRIENDS, NEW FRIENDS! LET'S PLAY, PLAY, PLAY!
NO! YOU'RE TRYING TO EAT US AND MY LITTLE BROTHER TOO!
?!?!?
HEE HEE, DRAGON IS TICKLING ANTO! HEE HEE!
HEY! THAT'S MY CATCH!
WHEEEEEE!

...
ANTO!
BUMP
WUMP
DID OLI SEE ANTO FLY?
NOW - CAN WE PLAY, PLAY, PLAY? MY NAME IS SEBASTIAN.
RAARGH!
CAN I PLAY WITH THEM, DADDY? CAN I PLAY WITH THEM, MOMMY?
SEBASTIAN, YOU ARE A MOCKERY TO DRAGONS EVERYWHERE.
DEAR, YOU SHOULD BE EATING THESE CREATURES, NOT PLAYING WITH THEM.
WHY DO YOU EVEN BOTHER? SEBASTIAN'S A LOSER - A FAILURE, PLAIN AND SIMPLE.

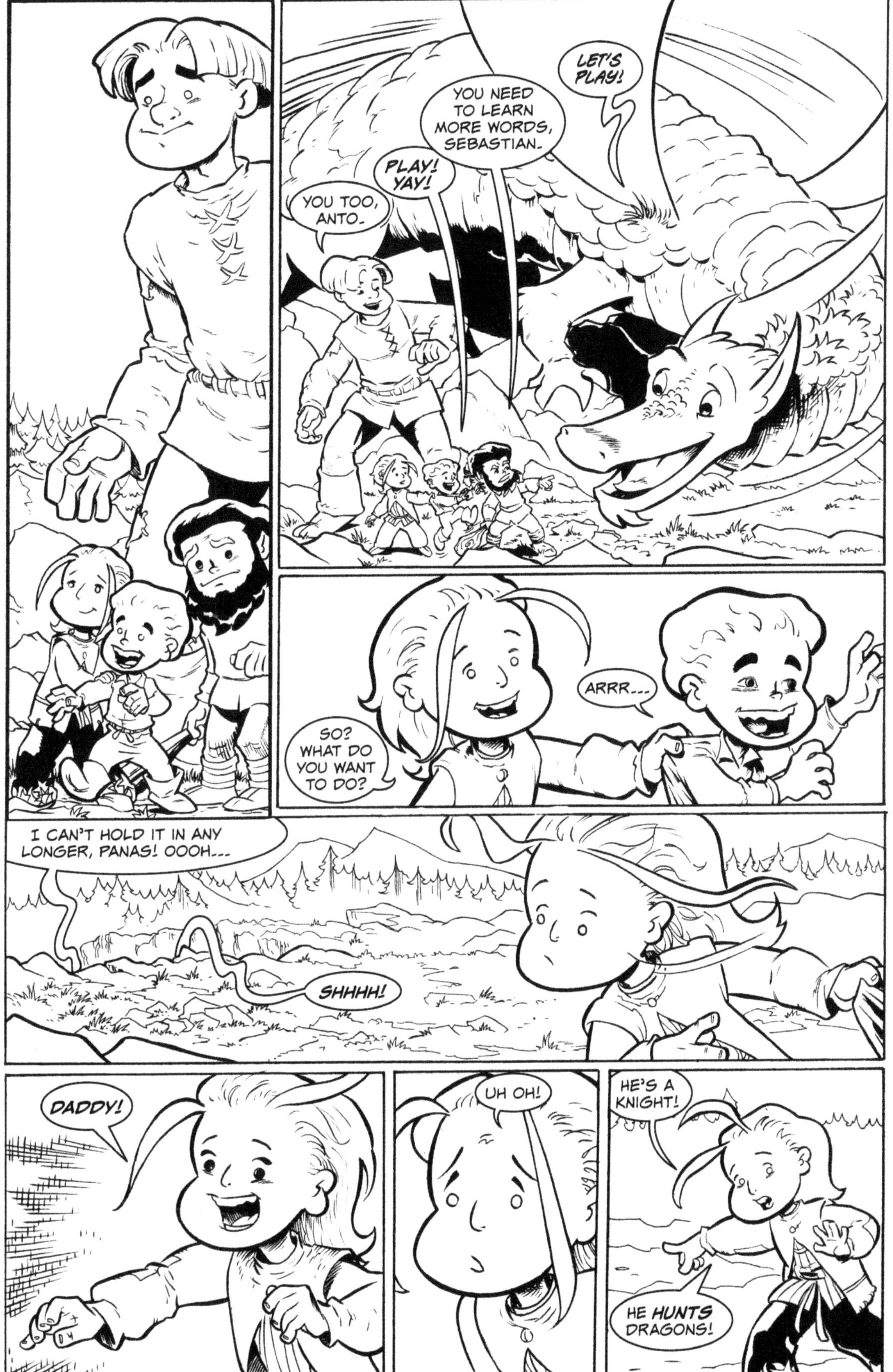

LET'S PLAY!
YOU NEED TO LEARN MORE WORDS, SEBASTIAN.
PLAY! YAY!
YOU TOO, ANTO.
ARRR...
SO? WHAT DO YOU WANT TO DO?
I CAN'T HOLD IT IN ANY LONGER, PANAS! OOOH...
SHHHH!
DADDY!
UH OH!
HE'S A KNIGHT!
HE HUNTS DRAGONS!

MOM, DAD - IF IT'S THOSE KNIGHTS FROM A COUPLE OF DAYS AGO - WE HAVE NOTHING TO WORRY ABOUT.
MY DAD - *SIR PANAS* - IS THE BEST DRAGON HUNTER IN THE LAND.
SIR PANAS THE DRAGONSLAYER?
OH DEAR - WE MUST HURRY!
LET'S GO, ROSCOE. WE SHALL FIGHT ANOTHER DAY.
GOODBYE, LOSER.
HEY...

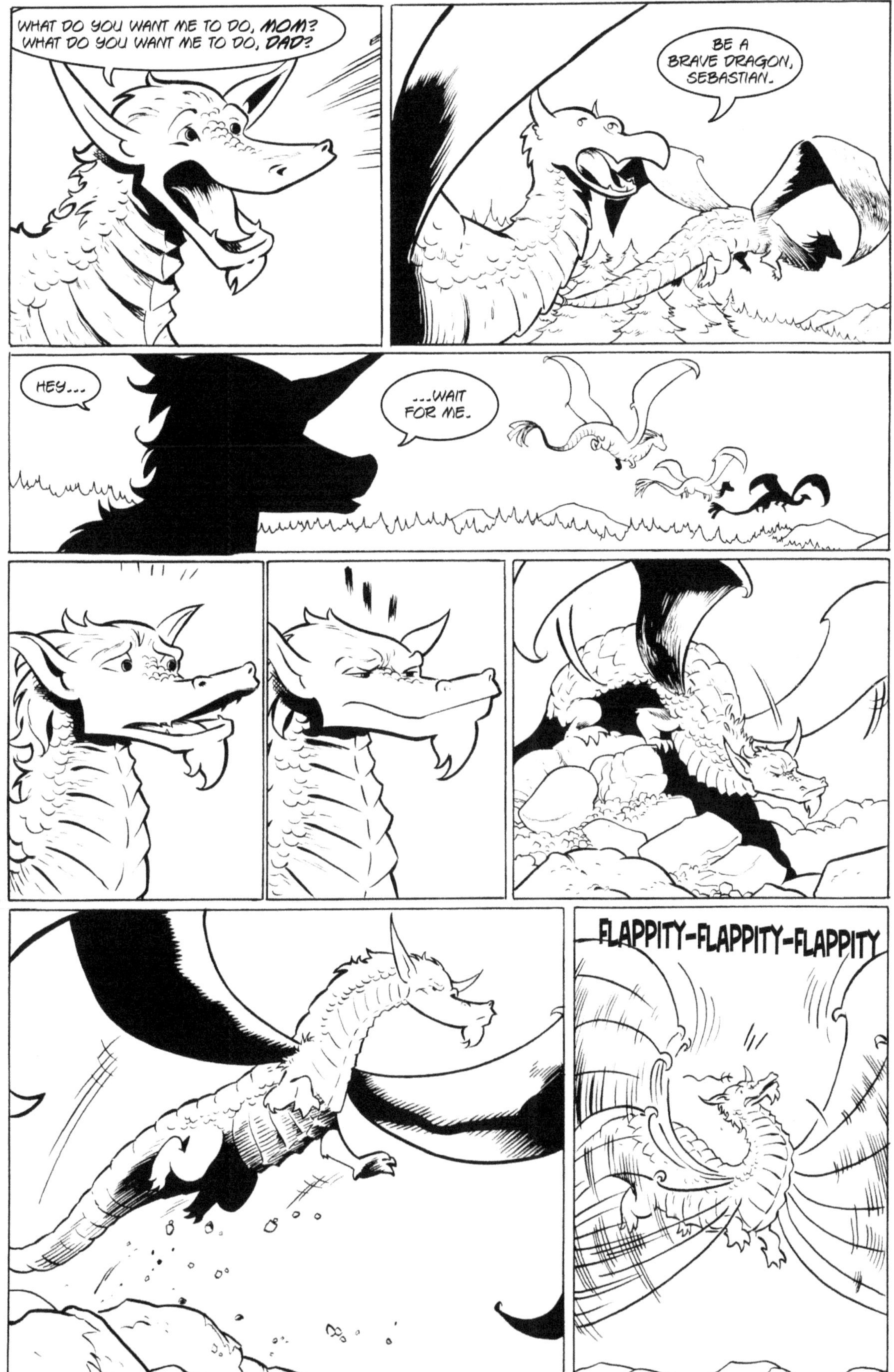
WHAT DO YOU WANT ME TO DO, MOM? WHAT DO YOU WANT ME TO DO, DAD?
BE A BRAVE DRAGON, SEBASTIAN.
HEY...
...WAIT FOR ME.
FLAPPITY-FLAPPITY-FLAPPITY

FLAPPITY-FLAPPITY-FLAPPITY-FLAPPITY-FLAPPITY-FLAPPITY-FLAP...
YIP
WOOMPF
OH NO! HE CAN'T FLY!

I THINK I HEARD SOMETHING OVER THIS WAY. QUIET, EVERYONE...
OH NO! HERE COMES YOUR DAD!
MMF! UGH!

DADDY!
ANTO! YOU'RE OKAY! THANK--- NO, WAIT!
YAY!
DAAADDDDDYYYYY
ANTO!!
OOPS.
HEY, THE KID'S OKAY.

!??!?!
A-YA
HI, DADDY! DO IT AGAIN! AGAIN!
MUMMMBLE GRUMBLE...
OLIANNA? BRADLEY? WHAT ARE YOU DOING HERE? WHY AREN'T YOU AT SCHOOL?
!!

WHAT DO YOU HAVE TO SAY FOR YOURSELF?
WAS IT THIS TROLL'S IDEA?
THE NAME IS THOMAS, SIR.
ANTO, DON'T EVER RUN AWAY FROM ME AGAIN, UNDERSTAND?
AND WHAT WERE YOU THINKING LEAVING SCHOOL, OLIANNA?
IT WAS THAT BULLY, DAD. I GOT DETENTION BECAUSE OF HIM.
SO SKIPPING SCHOOL WAS YOUR ANSWER?
IT SEEMED LIKE A GOOD IDEA AT THE TIME.
WELL, IT WASN'T
SNIFF
SNIFF
UH-OH.
SNIFF

?!
SNIFF
SNIFF
HMMMMM...
DID YOU USE YOUR YOU-KNOW-WHAT, OLI?
UMM... NO.
HMMMMM...
GULP
WAITA...
DID YOU GUYS..?
UH - WE TOLD YOU WE COULDN'T WAIT!
UMM, WE GOTTA GO.
WE'LL BE RIGHT BACK.

WHAT A WASTE OF A DAY, PAUL...
YEAH, NO DRAGONS - BUT AT LEAST THE KIDS ARE SAFE.
OLI, IS DRAGON STILL...
SHH! I THINK HE'S FOLLOWING.
KA-RACK
DID YOU HEAR SOMETHING?
I DIDN'T.
NO.

HMM... COULDA SWORN I HEARD SOMETHING.
PSST, WHERE'S YOUR HELMET?
HEAR THAT?
I DIDN'T HEAR ANYTHING.
ME NEITHER.
!??!?!
BUT...!
HMMF!
HUNH, HUNH? WHERE'S YOUR HELMET?
THERE!

THERE WHAT?
YEAH, ARE YOU OKAY, COPPER?
BUT...
WHERE'D IT GO? WHERE'D IT GO? DID YOU LOSE IT?
YAAAA!
I'M BEING HAUNTED!
RIGHT. HAUNTED.
BY HIS OWN INEPTITUDE, MAYBE.
HE'S ALMOST REACHED THE HORSES.
TEE HEE
HEE HEE
HEE HEE
HAHAHA
HEEHEEHEE

Later, after a million apologies...
THIS WILL NOT HAPPEN AGAIN. ESPECIALLY AFTER MY WIFE GETS THROUGH WITH HER, I PROMISE YOU.
I'LL KEEP AN EYE ON HER AND HER FRIENDS. AND CHAD AS WELL.
NOW GO ALONG AND PLAY - AND PLAY NICE!
Later, the kids start up a game of tag.

HEH
HEH
AAAA!
OOOF!
TAG!
YOU'RE IT!
THAT JERK!
WE OUGHT TO...
HAR HAR.
GRRR
...CAN'T DO ANYTHING.

HAHA! CAN'T CATCH ME!
HEEE HEE HEE
WAP!
YAAAAAAAAAAAAAA

TAG!
YOU'RE IT!
NO FAIR!
YOU CHEATED!
STOP YOUR WHINING, CHAD, AND LEAVE IT FOR DETENTION AFTER SCHOOL!
OLIANNA, NO DETENTION FOR YOU TODAY. CHAD DESERVES ONE ALL BY HIMSELF.
NOW, EVEN THOUGH YOU TRIED TO SKIP SCHOOL, I'M LETTING ALL OF YOU OFF EASY TODAY.

YOU'LL BE DOING SOME CHORES FOR ME DURING RECESS TOMORROW INSTEAD. MAYBE EVEN SOME LINES ON THE CHALKBOARD TOO.
I'LL BE WATCHING ALL OF YOU SO MAY I SUGGEST BEING ON YOUR BEST BEHAVIOR. NEXT TIME, I WON'T BE SO MERCIFUL.

HEE! HEE!
THANKS FOR YOUR HELP, SEBASTIAN.
FUN! FUN! FUN!
YOU'LL BE OKAY OUT HERE?
COZY! COZY! COZY!
GOT TO FIND MY FAMILY! MOMMY, DADDY, ROSCOE!
I'LL HELP YOU FIND THEM, SEBASTIAN. DON'T WORRY.
OLIANNA! GET TO BED THIS INSTANT! OR HAVE YOU NOT BEEN IN ENOUGH TROUBLE FOR ONE DAY?
COMING MOM!
GOOD NIGHT, SEBASTIAN. WE'LL PLAY TOMORROW.
OKAY, OLI.
OBOY. OBOY.
I CAN'T WAIT, WAIT, WAIT!
PLAY TOMORROW.
WHEN'S TOMORROW?

GROWING UP
ENCHANTED
SERRA
08
GROWING UP ENCHANTED

GROWING UP
ENCHANTED
SERRA 08
ANTO
BULLY
TROLL
PANAS
BENA
OLIANNA

www.ingramcontent.com/pod-product-compliance
Ingram Content Group UK Ltd.
Pitfield, Milton Keynes, MK11 3LW, UK
UKHW051126260726
13967UKWH00010B/2893